Flow Chart of Revelation

I0159469

End Time Judgments

■ ■ ■

By Prince Handley

University of Excellence Press

Copyright © 2009 by Prince Handley
All Rights Reserved.
UNIVERSITY OF EXCELLENCE PRESS

ISBN-13: 978-0692238875
ISBN-10: 0692238875

Printed in the U.S.A.
Second Edition

✠

The only End Time flow chart you need

TABLE OF CONTENTS

INTRODUCTION

This book is a sequential–**written**–flowchart of the judgments in *The Book of Revelation*. It is **not a pictorial chart**; and it is **designed that way purposely** to avoid confusion. There are lots of "charts" and pictorial representations which are confusing. This book attempts to avoid that.

What is needed is a **simplistic** "walk through" of the events that will take place during the End Times. The **purpose** of this book is to provide the following:

- Easy to understand flow of the End Times
- Aid to help you mentally picture events
- Method to store these events mentally
- Repeat "walk thru reviews" for clarification
- Tool to help you teach the End Times
- Inspiration to encourage you and others
- Challenge you to do NEW things for God

You can not only **know the news in advance …** you can **visualize it mentally** so that you can **recall it from memory** to walk through the events whenever you want to **…** plus, you can **teach Last Days events** to others.

Flow Chart
of
Revelation

■ ■ ■

End Time
Judgments

This book, *Flow Chart of Revelation*, focuses on the **judgments** that will be unleashed on Planet Earth during the end times.

Have you ever wondered what it would be like if you could know the news in advance? You know, not like for a week or two, but for the rest of man's time on earth.

Think how God could use if you had all this information! Well, God has already made it available in "The Revelation" to John (the last book in the New Testament of the Holy Bible). Actually, it is the revelation of Jesus Christ as he made these things known to his servant John. [Revelation 1:1.]

The Bible promises in Revelation 1:3 that you will be blessed if you **read** this book (The Revelation), or if you **listen** to, and **obey** the words of this message of prophecy. It is one of the easiest books in the Holy Bible to outline:

Chapter 1: The vision: what John saw—and what would happen in his time and in the future.

Chapters 2-3: Message to the seven churches. Things which would happen in John's time.

Chapter 4: Future events: things that will happen in the future.

Chapter 5: Shows a scroll in the hand of the one who sits on the throne; but no man in Heaven or earth is found who is worthy to break the seven seals on the scroll and open it. Then there is one who is worthy to open the scroll and look inside - it is the **Lion from Judah's tribe** who is worthy: the great descendant of David (Jesus, the Messiah of Israel).

Why is he found worthy? [Verse 9.] By His blood He bought men for God from every tribe, language, people, and nation.

He died to purchase us for God; **His BLOOD paid the price!**

INTRO

The End Time Judgments start in **Chapter 6 of the *Book of Revelation***.

That is what we will study in this book:

Flow Chart of Revelation: End Time Judgments.

So grab your Bible and follow along. Turn to the *Book of Revelation*. Throughout this book we will make references so you will know where to look.

Chapter 6 describes what happens when the Lamb breaks open the **first six** of the seven seals. What happens when the first six seals are opened.

BRIEF INFO

There are **seven (7) Seals**. The seventh (7th) Seal contains **seven (7) Trumpets**. The seventh

(7th) Trumpet contains **seven (7) Bowls (or, vials) of God's wrath**.

CAUTION

You will need this information in the future days for friends and relatives and others!

THE SEALS

Seal #1 - Rider on white horse - a bow and crown are given to him. He conquers. Notice: No arrows are given, showing he conquers with peace! Does not have to fight.

Seal #2 - Rider on red horse - world war (men kill each other); he has a large sword.

Seal #3 - Rider on black horse; has a pair of scales in his hand. A quart of wheat being sold for a whole day's wages shows great famine.

QUICK REVIEW

Seal #1 shows a person who conquers the world without war (he is given a crown). This leader will probably have a lot of military armament (a bow), but does not need to use it (has no arrows). **Seal #2** shows a world war; and **Seal #3** a famine. Read the details of the seals following.

Seal #4 - Rider on a pale horse; his name is "Death" and "Hades" follows him.

"And when he had opened the fourth seal, I heard the voice of the fourth beast say, Come and see.

And I looked, and behold a pale horse: and his name that sat on him was Death, and Hell followed with him. And power was given unto them over **the fourth part of the earth**, to kill with **sword,** and with **hunger,** and with **death,** and with the **beasts** of the earth." [Revelation 6:7-8]

One-fourth (25%) of the earth's population is killed by the four judgments in Seal #4:

- Sword (war, fighting, and terrorism)
- Famine (lack of food, along with drought and global warming)
- Disease (pestilence and pandemics: like AIDS, Ebola, anthrax, smallpox, swine flu)
- Wild animals (beasts) – No animal control

Only 75% of the world's population remains!

Seal #5 - Souls of saved people under the altar who had been killed for speaking God's Word and for witnessing about Messiah (Christ), not only in previous times, but also in this period of the End Times we are studying in the book!

Seal #6 - Violent earthquakes. The sun is black and the moon is red as blood. Stars fall from the sky and the sky disappears. The mountains and islands move from their place. People hide themselves in caves and rocks. [Next: Seal #7 opens up the 7 Trumpets (in Chapter 8).]

NOTICE

Chapter Seven is a "parenthesis" between Chapter 6 and Chapter 8 and describes two different scenes: one on earth, and the other in Heaven.

On earth, 144,000 Jewish servants of God are marked in their foreheads (to protect them from harm). In Heaven, there is a crowd so great no one can number the people; they are from every nation, tribe, people, and language.

Who are the people dressed in white robes in Chapter 7? [See verses 13 and 14.]

Those who have come safely through the great persecution, or those who washed their robes and made them white in the Lamb's blood.

Chapter 8 starts where Chapter 6 ended. The 7th seal is opened. **The 7th seal contains seven trumpets.** [See verse 2.] The first four of the seven trumpets are sounded in Chapter 8.

CAUTION

You will need this information in the future days for friends and relatives and others!

NOTE: The first four trumpets were judgments upon **natural objects**: one-third of the earth burnt (trees and grass), one-third of the sea and sea life (and ships) destroyed; one-third of the rivers and springs poisoned; and one-third of the sun, moon, and stars darkened. You can see how they will hurt man's food supply (the earth); his distribution of products (ships and sea); his water supply (rivers and springs); and his work, or production (loss of light by which to travel or work).

There are three trumpets left to sound which are known as three horrors or "woes".

Chapter 9 describes the first horror (Trumpet #5) and the second horror (Trumpet #6).

A REVIEW OF THE SEALS

Seal #1 - Rider on white horse - a bow and crown are given to him. He conquers. Notice: No arrows are given, showing he conquers with peace! This "rider" does not have to fight.

Seal #2 - Rider on red horse - world war (men kill each other); he has a large sword.

Seal #3 - Rider on black horse; has a pair of scales in his hand. A quart of wheat being sold for a whole day's wages shows great famine.

Seal #4 - Rider on a pale horse; his name is "Death" and "Hades" follows him

One-fourth (25%) of the earth's population is killed by four judgments:

- Sword (war, fighting, and terrorism)
- Famine (lack of food, along with drought and global warming)
- Disease (pestilence: like AIDS, Ebola, anthrax, smallpox, swine flu)
- Wild animals (beasts)

Only 75% of the world's population remains.

Seal #5 - Souls of saved people under the altar who had been killed for speaking God's Word and for witnessing about Christ.

Seal #6 - Violent earthquakes. The sun is black and the moon is red as blood. Stars fall from the sky and the sky disappears. The mountains and islands move from their place. People hide themselves in caves and rocks. [Next: Seal #7 opens up the 7 Trumpets.]

As mentioned previously, **Chapter 8 starts where Chapter 6 ended**. The 7th seal is opened. **The 7th seal contains seven trumpets**. [See verse 2.] The first four of the seven trumpets are sounded in Chapter 8.

THE TRUMPETS

Trumpet #1 - Hail stones and fire mixed with blood poured on earth. **One-third of the trees and grass are burned.**

Trumpet #2 - Burning mountain (meteorite?) is thrown into the sea. One-third of the sea is turned into blood. **One-third of the creatures on the sea die and one-third of the ships are destroyed.**

Trumpet #3 - Burning star named "Bitterness" (or, "Wormwood") is thrown into the rivers, streams, and springs. **One-third of waters become bitter and many die.**

Trumpet #4 - One-third of the sun, moon, and stars are darkened. **There is no light for one-third of on the night and day.**

The four Trumpet judgments just described are upon natural objects:

- Earth;
- Sea (and ships);
- Rivers and springs; and,
- Sun, moon, and stars.

You can see how they will hurt:

- Man's **food supply** (the earth);
- Man's **distribution of products** (ships and sea);
- Man's **water supply** (rivers and springs); and,
- Man's **work, or production** (loss of light to work or travel).

The next two judgments are upon **people** (NOT the natural objects like above).

As mentioned previously, there are three trumpets left to sound which are known as three horrors or "woes". Chapter 9 describes the first horror (Trumpet #5) and the second horror (Trumpet #6).

Trumpet #5 - 1st Horror (or, Woe) - Locusts with the power of scorpions torture those who do not have the mark of God's seal on their foreheads for five months. The people will want to die, but cannot.

Trumpet #6 - 2nd Horror (or, Woe) - Army of 200 million kills one-third of mankind with fire, smoke, and sulphur. People still do not repent. Now, only 50 percent (one half) of the world's population remains (see Seal #4). People still do NOT repent of worshipping demons and idols, nor of murder, drugs, fornication, and theft. This second horror (woe) continues into Chapter 11 **until the 7th trumpet** is sounded.

Next: **Trumpet #7** will open up in Chapter 11 – it opens up (contains) the seven Bowls (or, Vials) of God's wrath.

NOTE "A": Unlike the first four trumpets, where judgment is directed against **natural objects**, the 5th and 6th trumpet judgments are against **people**.

NOTE "B": **Only one-half of the earth's population will be left at this time**. One-fourth of the population was destroyed in Revelation 6:8, the 4th seal. This leaves three-fourths, or 75%, one-third of which is destroyed in Revelation 9:18.

NOTE "C": Men still do NOT repent of their murders, magic, immorality, or stealing. (Revelation 9:21.) **Magic in this verse includes drugs (or, narcotics)**, sometimes accompanied by witchcraft. We know this because of the original Greek word used here for magic or, sorcery is the word "pharmakeia."

Chapter 10 tells of an angel, with one foot on the land and one on the sea, who announces there will be no more delay. When the 7th trumpet sounds, God will begin to accomplish his secret plan. **Chapter 11 tells of two witnesses who are street preachers**. They proclaim God's message for 3½ years. After they finish their message, the beast out of the bottomless pit (Satan) is allowed to kill them.

What will the people of earth do when the two street preachers are killed? [See Revelation 11:10.] Celebrate and send presents to one another. After 3½ days, a life-giving breath from God enters the dead preachers and they stand up. What happens then? [Read about this in Revelation 11:11-12.]

People who see them are afraid. [They will probably watch from around the world by satellite broadcast or similar communications.] **A voice from heaven says: "Come up here!"** The street preachers then go up to heaven in a cloud.

Then there is another earthquake (the third, so far), and a tenth of the city is destroyed (7,000 people are killed).

How do we know that this city where the street preachers are preaching is Jerusalem? [See verse 8.] It is the city where the Lord was nailed to the cross.

This is the end of the second horror, or woe. Then **the 7th angel sounds his trumpet** (start of the third horror) and announces that the power to rule over the world belongs to our Lord and to his Messiah: the Messiah of Israel, Yeshua HaMashiach (Jesus the Anointed One). Then, another earthquake!

We will not study what happens as a result of **Trumpet #7** being sounded until Chapter 15. The three chapters between [12, 13, and 14] will show us events that will happen meanwhile.

Chapter 12 describes a woman (the nation Israel) who gives birth to a son, Yeshua (Jesus). **We know that the woman who is described here represents Israel by the way she is described in this chapter and also by the description in verse 1**. In the Old Testament, Genesis 37:9-11, Joseph had a dream in which his 11 brothers were described as stars. These 12 brothers were the heads of the 12 tribes of Israel. Joseph's parents were the sun and moon in this dream.

The dragon, who is the Devil (see verse 9), stood in front of the woman to devour (eat up) the child as soon as it was born (verse 4). This is how Satan used King Herod when Jesus was born. **Herod had all the young male babies, two years and under killed; but Jesus' parents took him to Egypt until Herod died**, and so Jesus was safe.

Verse 5 of Chapter 12 tells how Jesus was born and then taken to God and to his throne. These events (the woman who gave birth to a son, and the son going up to God) are NOT future events; they have already happened, as you know. However, they are important events and the Holy Spirit had them recorded in Scripture because they help us to see why Satan hates the Jewish people. **Why does Satan hate the Jews?** [See Revelation 12:13.]

▉ Because a Jewish woman gave birth to the (male) child Jesus, who defeated Him.

■ Because he (the devil) was defeated and thrown out of Heaven.

■ Also, because the Word of God, the Holy Bible, was written by Jews.

You see, it was the BLOOD of Jesus on the cross that defeated Satan. **The devil hates the people of Israel, because it was through Jewish ancestry (or, family lines) that Jesus was born**.

There will be a time of great persecution for the Jews in the future. **It will last for 3 ½ years =** 1,260 days = 42 months. [See verses 6 and 14] **It will be worse than the Holocaust under Nazi Germany!**

Chapter 13 describes a beast coming up **out of the sea**. Who gives him his power? [Re. 13:2.] The dragon (Satan) gives the beast **out of the sea** his power. The beast **out of the sea** is the anti-Christ leader who will be the leader chosen by the New World Governance.

People will worship the dragon, who is Satan, and the beast. [See verse 4.] This beast out of the sea is the coming world ruler described here in Chapter 13, verses 5-8, and in other places of the Holy Bible. Who will NOT worship the beast?

Everyone whose name has been written before the world began in the *Book of Life* (the Book of the Living) that belongs to the Lamb who was killed (Yeshua, or Jesus) will NOT worship the beast. [Those who have been written in the Book of Life of the Lamb slain from the foundation of the world.]

This coming world ruler is also known as the "false-Messiah", or the "anti-Christ". He [seemingly] dies and then [it appears as if] his deadly wound is healed.

Another beast is seen coming up **out of the earth**. [Look at verse 11.] **He is the false prophet**. He causes people to worship the first beast (the anti-Christ) and **to make an IMAGE** of him. Then, the false prophet (seemingly) gives life to the IMAGE of the first beast.

The IMAGE could be any of the following:

- Holographic image
- Robot with Artificial Intelligence (AI)
- Android that is a living AI of the Beast
- Virtual Reality Avatar with AI of the Beast

It could well be that IF the **false prophet** is from the Islamic Caliphate, that those who will NOT take the mark of the beast are **beheaded as is common practice in Islamic countries**, particularly where Sharia Law is in practice.

NOTICE TWO THOUGHT TWISTERS

THOUGHT TWISTER #1 – The **false prophet** could **possibly** be Jewish. Neither the false prophet nor the false messiah will appear with "horns and a pitchfork." The devil is subtle, cunning and a mega-deceiver. What if the false prophet were a rabbi: a world renowned peace leader?

THOUGHT TWISTER #2 – The **false messiah** could **possibly** be Jewish. Some early church fathers believed this. A charismatic Israeli leader—especially a military leader who defeats Islamic forces and then legislates for peace—will have an automatic inroad, especially favored by Christians and Jews.

These two "thought twisters" are possibilities—maybe NOT probabilities—but they are plausible. Consider, also, that the Prophet Daniel said concerning the **false messiah** (the anti-christ) that: *"He shall regard neither the God of his fathers nor the desire of women, nor regard any god, for he shall exalt himself above them all."* (Daniel 11:37)

The above scripture passage from the Tanakh **may** show that the **anti-christ (false messiah) comes from a line of religious ancestors**.

The **false prophet**, who will be the religious head of the world, forces ALL people to have a mark placed on their right hands or in their foreheads. No one can buy or sell unless they have his mark: the mark is a name, or the number that represents the beast's name. What is the number of the beast, the mark which people will be forced to take? [Revelation 13:18.]

The number is: "666."

WARNING

When this happens, God's wrath will be poured out upon all who take this mark.

Warn your friends and relatives NOT to do it!

Chapter 14 tells that the great Babylon has fallen who influenced all nations with immoral lust. All who worship the beast and its image, and receive this mark will be tormented in fire with no relief forever.

Chapter 15 starts where Chapter 11 ends: at the 7th trumpet.

QUICK REVIEW

Just for review, remember that there are seven seals. Seal #7 contains seven trumpets; and now we will see that **Trumpet #7 contains seven bowls of God's wrath** (or, the seven last plagues).

Chapter 16 describes the **seven last plagues (the seven bowls of God's wrath)**.

THE BOWLS, OR VIALS

Bowl #1 - Painful sores on those who have taken the "Mark of the Beast" and who worship his image.

Bowl #2 - The sea becomes like the blood of a dead person. Every living creature in the sea dies.

Bowl #3 - Rivers and waters become blood. An angel says, "This is a righteous judgment because people on earth have shed the blood of God's people and of the prophets who speak to them."

Bowl #4 - The sun burns men with fiery heat. They curse God and do not repent.

Bowl #5 - Darkness over the kingdom of the Beast, the Anti-Christ. Men bite their tongues because of their pain and they curse God.

Bowl #6 - The Euphrates River in Iraq is dried up to make a way for the kings from the East to make war. Three (3) unclean spirits (demons) come out of the false trinity:

- A demon comes out of the mouth of **the devil** (the "dragon);
- A demon comes out of the mouth of **the beast**, the Anti-Christ; and,
- A demon comes out of the mouth of **the false prophet** (the religious leader).

These demons perform miracles and go out to the kings over the whole earth to bring them together for the war on the Great Day of the Almighty God (Armageddon).

Bowl #7 - worst earthquake of all:

- Babylon is split into three (3) parts;
- Cities of the nations are destroyed;
- All islands and mountains disappear; and,
- Hail stones weighing up to 100 pounds fall on people (the people curse God).

The cities of the nations, and Babylon, represent the centers of the power and influence of Satan, the beast, the false prophet, and all their anti-Messiah partners. They all fall!

Remember: false-Messiah is also anti-Messiah! He loses. We win through Messiah Jesus! Go tell others!

CAUTION

You will need this information in the future days for friends and relatives and others!

Chapter 17 describes the great city Babylon as a prostitute. This city causes the leaders and people of the nations to be influenced with immorality. (Re. 17:2.) **This great city will be destroyed by the 10 nation-state leaders** (the 10 kings or "horns" of Revelation 17:12). These

10 leaders of nations are finally given authority to rule at the same time (one hour, figuratively) with the beast.

What are two ways people will be able to know, or identify, this city in the future? [Verse 6 and verse 18.] **1.** Responsible for killing God's people who had been loyal to Jesus. **2.** The city will dominate the kings (or, leaders) of the earth. **NOTE:** See additional notes below for more ways to identify the city.

IMPORTANT

Study Prince Handley's book, Babylon the Bitch: Enemy of Israel for details and intel on Babylon.

NOTE: There are seven (7) ways you will be able to identify this city in the future.

SEVEN WAYS TO IDENTIFY BABYLON

- Influences world trade;
- Deceives all nations by its witchcraft and narcotics;
- Rules over the leaders of the nations;
- Responsible for murdering Christians and Messianic Jews; and;
- Causes leaders and people of the nations to be influenced with immoral lust;
- Key distributor of pornography, sexual trade, and idolatry;
- It is a seaport city.

DISCUSSION

See if you can find in the *Book of Revelation* where the seven descriptors are mentioned.

Chapter 18 actually describes the detailed fall announced in Chapter 17. Notice that there are **27 commodities** listed as being traded in and from this city. That is **another reason we know it is a literal city** ... and not just a religious system. Babylon, the great city, will be hit with plagues in one day and burnt with fire. The businessmen of the earth who trade with her, and who are made rich by that commerce, will be sad because in one hour the city loses everything. **Why will the city be punished?** [See Revelation 18:23, 24.] Because the blood of prophets and God's people is found in the city.

NOTE: In verse 23, we see that the city used magic, or sorcery, to deceive the people of the world. Magic in this verse includes drugs (or, narcotics), sometimes accompanied by witchcraft. As discussed previously, we know this because of the original Greek word used for magic (or,sorcery): "pharmakeia."

Chapter 19 shows the King of Kings and Lord of Lords appearing from Heaven and the armies of Heaven are with him. [Re. 19:14-16.] The kings (or, the leaders) of the earth and their armies gather together to fight against the Lord and his army.

The beast and the false prophet are thrown alive into the lake of fire that burns with sulfur; and the armies of the earth are killed with a sharp sword that comes out of the mouth of the Lord. [Revelation 19:19-20.]

In Chapter 20 we see that Satan is bound for 1,000 years - at the end of the 1,000 years he will be loosed for a little while. Those who were killed for the testimony (or, the truth) of Jesus, and for the Word of God, ... and had not worshipped the beast or his image ... and had NOT taken his mark ... live and rule as kings with Christ for 1,000 years.

After the 1,000 years, Satan is loosed a little while to deceive the nations of the world. The armies of the nations surround the city that God loves (Jerusalem), but fire comes down from Heaven and destroys them.

The devil (Satan) will be cast into the lake of fire and sulfur ... where the beast and false prophet already have been for the 1,000 years during which Satan was bound. How long will they all be tormented? [Read Revelation 20:10.]

Day and night forever and ever without end! [Note: in the original Greek language in which the New Testament was written, it shows the torment will never cease.]

Next, is the Great White Throne judgment. Whoever does not have their name in the Book of Life is thrown into the lake of fire. [Read verses 11 through 15 in Revelation Chapter 20.]

Chapter 21 describes a New Heaven and New Earth. The holy city, New Jerusalem, comes down out of Heaven.

In **Chapter 22**, Messiah Jesus says, *"Listen, I am coming to you soon!"*

ANNOUNCEMENT

We recommend you obtain the companion books to this book in the **Prophecy Series** by Prince Handley. You will want to obtain, ***Prophetic Calendar for Israel and the Nations.*** This book is **a prophetic outlook through 2023**. Another must read in the series is ***Map of the End Times***, which focuses in detail on the coordination of the End Times events with information pertaining to the New Global Governance and all it involves: finance, globalism and religion. Learn **new**, updated, never before exposed tips and **secrets of geopolitical interrelationships**. How they will evolve in the End Times. Also, **intel regarding the IMAGE of The Beast: what it is.**

And, you need ***Babylon the Bitch: Enemy of Israel***, which identifies specifically WHO and WHAT Babylon is. This book discusses in detail how the enemy of Israel and all of God's People—Satan—will try to juxtaposition Babylon (a real city) in opposition to Jerusalem: both spiritually and physically.

Most people do NOT realize that **the KEY enemy of Israel has clandestine architectural and strategic**—as well as spiritual—**plans against Israel**. Plans that **include much more than Iran or ISIS or the UN.** This book covers the next—**the worst**—Jewish Holocaust. Plus … the only game plan **that will work** for Israel.

You will definitely need this information in the future!

Now that you know you WIN … go tell others. You might want to move to Israel and help teach the 144,000 Jewish evangelists who are being set apart and called by God at this very time!

UNIVERSITY OF EXCELLENCE PRESS
Los Angeles ■ London ■ Tel Aviv

LIVE A LIFE OF EXCELLENCE

✝

Schedule seminars with Prince Handley:
princehandley@gmail.com

Study these companion books in the
Prophecy Series by Prince Handley:

Map of the End Times

Babylon the Bitch – Enemy of Israel

Prophetic Calendar for Israel & the Nations Thru 2023

AVAILABLE AT AMAZON AND OTHER BOOK STORES

UNIVERSITY OF EXCELLENCE PRESS
Los Angeles ▮ London ▮ Tel Aviv

See next page for **Other Books** by Prince Handley

OTHER BOOKS BY PRINCE HANDLEY

- Map of the End Times
- How to Do Great Works
- Flow Chart of Revelation
- Action Keys for Success
- Health and Healing Complete Guide to Wholeness
- Prophetic Calendar for Israel & the Nations: Thru 2023
- Healing Deliverance
- How to Receive God's Power with Gifts of the Spirit
- Healing for Mental and Physical Abuse
- Victory Over Opposition and Resistance
- Healing of Emotional Wounds
- How to Be Healed and Live in Divine Health
- Healing from Fear, Shame and Anger
- How to Receive Healing and Bring Healing to Others
- New Global Strategy: Enabling Missions
- The Art of Christian Warfare
- Success Cycles and Secrets
- New Testament Bible Studies (A Study Manual)
- Babylon the Bitch – Enemy of Israel
- Resurrection Multiplication – Miracle Production
- Faith and Quantum Physics – Your Future
- Conflict Healing – Relational Health
- Decision Making 101 – Know for Sure

AVAILABLE AT AMAZON AND OTHER BOOK STORES

UNIVERSITY OF EXCELLENCE PRESS
Los Angeles ■ London ■ Tel Aviv